30 Days on:

Changing Your World

30 Days on:

Changing Your World

a journal companion

Pr. sean lumsden

NoOffSwitichPress

Spokane, Washington

© 2021 by Sean Lumsden

All rights reserved. No part of this publication may be reproduced, stored in a retrieval system, or transmitted in any form or by any means, electronic, mechanical, photocopying, recording or otherwise, without prior permission of the publisher.

This book is available for bulk sales, promotions, premiums, or fundraisers. Please contact the publisher at NoOffSwitch@Outlook.com for more information.

Abide in Me, and I in you. As the branch cannot bear fruit of itself unless it abides in the vine, so neither can you unless you abide in Me. I am the vine; you are the branches; he who abides in Me and I in him, he bears much fruit,

    John 15.4

Contents

Day 1: Introduction — 6

Day 2: Get to Rome — 8

Day 3: Paul's Story — 10

Day 4: Jesus Alone — 12

Day 5: Answering Objections — 14

Day 6: Articulating the Process — 16

Day 7: What is Your Rome? — 18

Day 8: 'We' Get to Rome — 20

Day 9: Expect Opposition — 22

Day 10: God Working in Spiritual Conflict — 24

Day 11: Waiting Longer — 26

Day 12: Wrong Season — 28

Day 13: Pastor Your Shipwreck- Before the Wreck — 30

Day 14: Be a Prophetic Voice — 32

Day 15: Expect Not to be Listened To — 34

Day 16: Bad to Worse — 36

Day 17: Peace in the Midst — 38

Day 18: Prevail in Prayer	40
Day 19: Know Whose You Are	42
Day 20: Assume Responsibility	44
Day 21: Deliver the Good and the Bad	46
Day 22: Hold on Tight	48
Day 23: Pastor Your Shipwreck	50
Day 24: God Never Promised the Boat	52
Day 25: It's OK to Just Survive	54
Day 26: Go Serve	56
Day 27: Expect...	58
Day 28 Shake it Off and Heal the City	60
Day 29: Love the Person Chained to You	62
Day 30: Bound is Just a State of Mind	64
Appendix 1: Why Journal?	66
Appendix 2: Which Bible	68
Appendix 3: Prayer Tips	70
Appendix 4: Agreements	74
About the Author	

Day 1: Introduction

My hero, Jerry Cook, was asked why he was a Pentecostal. "Because Jesus told me to change the world, and I need the power of the Spirit to do that!"

One of the most impacting books I read as a teenager was Ann Kiemel's "I'm out to change my world."

The other huge influence on my transformative teenage years was Keith Green. He famously sang, "Jesus commands us to go…it should be the exception if we stay."

And of course…Jesus Himself said: "Go into all the world and make disciples. Baptizing them in the name of the Father, the Son and the Holy Spirit. Teaching them to obey all I have commanded them."

If believers take Jesus seriously, we have quite a task ahead of us. So this booklet will talk about how we take the Great Commission seriously. Sadly, the American church is more about fulfilling the Great Omission or the Great Comfort-mission.

Comfort-mission… spell check doesn't like that…and neither does Jesus.

Historically, when Christians have been challenged to fulfill the great commission, this meant mission trips. Early Pentecostals would pack all their belongings into a casket so they would be prepared for their burial.

Over time, the mission passion moved toward learning how to witness. We had 'soul-winners' New Testaments and taught people how to walk the 'Romans Road' and shared with them the '4 Spiritual Laws.' If that wasn't enough, we read "Out of the Salt Shaker and Into the World." The Vineyard movement led the way with "Power Evangelism" then softened it up to "Conspiracy of Kindness."

The "Conspiracy of Kindness" moved into acts of service that churches could do for their neighborhood. Giving kids backpacks of school supplies or mowing the lawn at the local school.

All of these ideas can be powerful...but sadly, the American church has declined in its impact with each generation.

But...the good news is the same Spirit that raised Christ from the dead STILL lives in us and STILL can change our world.

How do we do this? Simple.

We 'Pastor our Shipwreck.'

What has your experience been with evangelism and discipleship in the past? Has it been successful?

Day 2: Get to Rome

Acts 25.24 Festus said: "King Agrippa... The whole Jewish community has petitioned me ... that he ought not to live any longer. 25 I found he had done nothing deserving of death, but because he made his appeal to the Emperor I decided to send him to Rome.

Christianity had to get to Rome. Jesus came from backwater Bethlehem and Nazareth. The title 'Jesus the Nazarene' is a slur equivalent to 'Jesus, the slack-jawed yokel.' When Jesus died in Jerusalem, He died in a regional center. But for Christianity to get around the world, it first had to get to the center of the world: Rome.

Paul had been a Pharisee who was killing Christians for their newfound faith. After He met Jesus on the road to Damascus, His life changed. The second half of the book of Acts is a series of conflicts between Paul and the religious and political leaders.

The Jews wanted Paul dead because he was preaching the crucified Christ and backing up the messages with astonishing works of power as Jesus did. He also angered the local business community by delivering a demon-possessed woman who they were exploiting for financial gain. Ultimately, the Jewish leaders take an oath to fast until they kill Paul.

Our story starts with Paul being tried before Festus. Because Paul was a Roman citizen, he had the legal right to have his case tried before Caesar in Rome. So even though Paul used every opportunity to tell his conversion story, in the back of his mind is the fact that his ultimate destiny was Rome: the center of the world.

Every believer has a 'Rome.' Every believer has a destiny in Jesus toward which their life will build. For Paul, he had to get Christianity to Rome. From Rome, traveling to the 'uttermost parts of the earth' could be realized. **This is how we change our world: The more we become like Jesus, the more God can use us to bring life and hope to those around us.** We become people with a calling on our life, and we watch as God opens miraculous door after miraculous door.

But...as we will see in this story, the enemy of our souls will become aggressive in trying to stop us on our journey. Paul will encounter a shipwreck on the way.

How do we change our world? We determine to get to Rome, we anticipate a shipwreck, and we pastor our shipwreck until everyone in our circle becomes a disciple. Discipleship is the only thing that has ever changed the world for the good. Hmmm...and isn't that what Jesus told us to do?

Have you ever sensed a destiny for your life?

Day 3: Paul's Story

Acts 26.13 as I was on the road, I saw a light from heaven... 15 "Then I asked, 'Who are you, Lord?' 'I am Jesus ... 17 I will rescue you from your own people and from the Gentiles. I am sending you to them 18 to open their eyes and turn them from darkness to light, and from the power of Satan to God, so that they may receive forgiveness of sins and a place among those who are sanctified by faith in me.'

Paul goes before the highest regional authority, King Agrippa, to present his case.

Addressing the king, Paul clarifies that his conflict with the Jews centers on the fact that Paul believes Jesus was the Messiah (or Christ) and that Jesus was raised from the dead. He is confident of this because he used to be one of the people now demanding his death! He tells Agrippa that he was on a journey to kill more Christians when Jesus appears to him.

Jesus appears in a blinding light and asks why Paul is persecuting Him through persecuting His followers.

Take a look at the passage above one more time. Do you notice how Jesus frames the discussion of salvation? **Jesus calls salvation a turning from the power of Satan and darkness to God and light**. Paul will reiterate this in Colossians when He says that Jesus has delivered us from the dominion of darkness to the kingdom of light.

Do you see the centrality of the spiritual battle in these comments? The active force of evil on earth is not something from which Jesus or Paul shies away. They hit this subject head-on. The rest of this story will show how this battle plays out in real-time.

Paul shared his testimony everywhere he could. He knew that as people heard of who he used to be, what Jesus did, and who he is now, people would respond, and lives would be changed. Note that Paul still could've rejected Jesus, but he didn't.

Your story has the same power. Sharing your faith is as simple as just telling people who you were, how Jesus intersected, and how you changed. You might be intimidated to share, but remember, in our society everyone is allowed their story. You don't have to agree, but people will be open to hear and process.

So this week, ask the Lord who you can share your story with. Someone told you their story and your life changed.

Reflect on your testimony. Who were you before Jesus, how did Jesus intercept your life and how is your life different now?

Day 4: Jesus Alone

25.22 I stand here and testify to small and great alike. I am saying nothing beyond what the prophets and Moses said would happen— 23 that the Messiah would suffer and, as the first to rise from the dead, would bring the message of light to his own people and to the Gentiles."

We're going to take a quick side trip to talk about sharing your faith. I have simplified the process to this: J-J-E-S-U-S. Jesus with an extra J for no extra charge.

This acrostic helps us remember that our main conversation is Jesus. Everyone has an issue or two with the church, but few people can disagree with Jesus. When you share your faith, always remember that Christianity is ONLY about agreeing with Jesus in your beliefs and behaviors. When you can strip away a person's problems with the church, you quickly see that they probably agree with Jesus on many subjects.

Muslims love Jesus. They believe He was the prophet who preceded Mohammad and will return to earth to rule with Mohammad. Hindus love Jesus. They see in Him an enlightened teacher who showed the power of a non-violent life. Buddhists love Jesus. They see Him as being one who is free from the trappings of this life and a great example of the eight-fold path.

Yet Jesus ONLY points to Himself. 'I am the way, the truth and the life. NO ONE comes to the Father but by Me (John 14.3).' When we share our faith, we should always point to Jesus and Jesus alone. **What people think about Jesus is the most important thought in their brain.** This is the only thought that contains the potential for an eternal destiny.

I also like to look at the three reasons people don't agree with Jesus: The first reason is they feel they are smarter than Jesus. They may not use these words, but at some level, disagreeing with Jesus to agree with someone else, or your own thinking, says you are smarter than Jesus.

The second reason is morality. If Jesus says, 'don't do that' and people want to 'do that,' on some level, they are saying they have a higher level of morality than Jesus.

The third reason is power. If someone doesn't feel they need Jesus in their life, they are subtly saying He doesn't bring any extra power that they need. They are strong enough as is and do not believe they will need any additional power in the afterlife.

In our world, the simple thought that 'God does not think like man' is a revolutionary thought. When people take elements from each philosophy and create their own belief structure, they are saying that their own reasoning is God. More on why I don't trust my brain tomorrow.

Reflect on 'Jesus alone' in witnessing.

Day 5: Answering Objections: J-J-E-S-U-S

25.24 At this point Festus interrupted Paul's defense. "You are out of your mind, Paul!" he shouted. "Your great learning is driving you insane."25 "I am not insane, most excellent Festus," Paul replied. "What I am saying is true and reasonable.

This entry will give you a good framework for answering objections.

So, let's look at the acrostic. **The first J is simple: Jerk-don't be one!** There are too many people who claim to be Christians and have no ethics or gentleness in their life. Don't be that person! I tell people at my church, don't tell others what church they attend until they are sure the person they are talking to feels loved by them.

Here is the amazing news: Everyone can serve. If you just live your life with a servant's heart and ask people 'what can I do for you?' on a regular basis, you will gain authority to speak into their lives. It may be a cliché, but it is a true point: People don't care what you know until they know that you care.

The second J is 'Just listen.' When you are having important discussions, be sure to let your friend tell you why they believe what they believe. Don't get defensive; don't feel you have to have all the answers. Listen, ask good questions, and be willing to get more information later.

E- Examine for hope. Listen especially, for where they place their hope. Their hope will point to the cry of their heart, and only Jesus can supply that! Do they put their hope on 'right living?'Or on not being 'as bad as Hitler?' (I always love that one... way to keep the standards high.) Ultimately, they will put their hope on their own ability to live without God.

S- Surprise with agreement. This is the one point I love! Tell them how their belief structure agrees with Jesus. Do they want 'peace of mind?' Jesus wants them to have that! Do they want to contribute to the betterment of the world? Jesus REALLY wants them to have that. Most people want a life marked with love, peace, and purpose. Jesus came to earth to give mankind all these things.

U- Uncover differences. Now things can get sticky. But remember, many of the differences are because people don't know the truth about Jesus. Just telling people God doesn't micro-manage the universe opens many doors. **When you clarify that all-powerful means all-resourceful and not all-controlling** you see lights go off in their brain. I always preface these points with 'you don't have to agree with me, but at least know what the Bible says before you disagree.'

Which of these six steps seems easiest and which one seems hardest?

Day 6: Articulating the Process

25.27 King Agrippa, do you believe the prophets? I know you do." 28 Then Agrippa said to Paul, "Do you think that in such a short time you can persuade me to be a Christian?" 29 Paul replied, "Short time or long—I pray to God that not only you but all who are listening to me today may become what I am, except for these chains."

Paul, on trial for his life, is still trying to get people to say yes to Jesus. This is the whole message of this booklet: while you are on your way to becoming more like Jesus, you are to take responsibility for the people in front of you. At our church, we like to call this 'loving the person in front of you.' You have a destiny from God, but you also have a responsibility to the person in front of you.

The final letter of our acrostic: S- Share your story. After you have listened and cleared up some differences, step in and share who you were before Jesus. Explain the forces that led you to convert. Feel free to share some struggles along the way, but most importantly, tell them honestly about your new life.

For me, I always come back to telling people how **my brain has been behind every bad decision I have ever made. I can't trust my own thinking and motivations** because my motivations are always focused on my comfort. I turn to Jesus because I am not smart enough, moral enough, or powerful enough to disagree.

When they are ready to move forward, explain to them that becoming a Christian is as easy as A, B, C.

A: Applying what Jesus did on the cross for your past and future. You are forgiven for your past and preparing yourself to agree with Jesus for your future.

B: Believe what Jesus believes about Himself (that He is God) and the Bible (the Bible is the word of God). You may not get everything at first, but you are choosing to grow in that direction.

C: Conspire to bring the love of Jesus to your world. As you agree with Jesus, you bring His peace and power into our world, making the world a better place for all.

Remember, someone in your world is close to accepting Jesus right now. Ask God who they are and how you can help.

Ask God, who in your world may be close to becoming a Christian?

Day 7: What is Your 'Rome?'

26. 30 The king rose, and with him the governor and Bernice and those sitting with them. 31 After they left the room, they began saying to one another, "This man is not doing anything that deserves death or imprisonment." 32 Agrippa said to Festus, "This man could have been set free if he had not appealed to Caesar."

Paul, just like Jesus, is freed from the Gentile judges. Yet both of them still have their greatest moment of destiny ahead. Jesus went to the cross; Paul went to Rome. At the beginning of this booklet, we looked at our destiny called 'Rome.' The Bible frequently talks about a time and or place of destiny. Whether it was Abraham having children and land, or the children of Israel having their promised land; God plans for His people to live a fulfilling life of provision and power.

Yet, most Christians never get to their 'Rome.' Why is that?

First, let's establish what destiny is. Destiny is you- Christlike. Paul says in Romans 8 that believers are predestined to Christlikeness, not merely salvation.

[handwritten: Destiny]
Your Rome is you living with the fruits of the spirit, the gifts of the Spirit and the power of the Spirit while loving the person in front of you. Its not a career, city, marital status or title. As you learn to love and live like

Jesus, all those things I've mentioned will be part of your Rome. But they are secondary to you walking in the character and power of Jesus.

And why is the power of Jesus necessary? Because He said it would be. He prophesied we would do greater things than He did (John 14.12-14) once we are empowered by the Spirit (Acts 1.8), if we seek His kingdom first (Matt. 6.33).

All these things may seem daunting, but remember, if we just seek His Kingdom and highest good for everyone (i.e., His righteousness), we will be on the right path. Just become obsessed with loving the person in front of you and doing to them as you would have done to you. This is the narrow path that Jesus tells us to strive to enter (Matt. 7.12-14).

As you walk down this path, you will be bearing the fruit of the Spirit that Paul promises. Love, Joy, Peace, Patience, Kindness, Goodness, Faithfulness, Gentleness, and Self-Control will grow into your character. Then as your character reflects Jesus, His power can flow through you unimpeded to those around you.

This is your destiny...your 'Rome.' Let's watch Paul walk into his.

Imagine your future if you *really* walked like Jesus.

Day 8: 'We' Get to Rome

Acts 27: When it was decided that we would sail for Italy, Paul and some other prisoners were handed over to a centurion named Julius... 2 We boarded a ship from ... and we put out to sea. 3 The next day we landed at Sidon...

Did you notice the pronoun shift? Now the story is being told as a 'we' story. Why has this changed? Luke, the author of Acts, has joined the boat.

As you get to your Rome, your journey will be joined by other believers who will stay close to your side and wish to become Jesus' disciple with you.

Many believers will recoil from this ominous task and ask, 'why would God want me to disciple ANYONE?' It is easy for us to get obsessed with what we don't have and who we aren't yet.

Please note the keyword 'yet.'

God only uses broken, hurting Christians to build His kingdom. Why? They are the only people who exist.

Being completely convinced of who you **aren't** is the first step in discipleship. But, radical discipleship starts the moment you realize that you can't but Jesus can through you. And He expects us to jump in and do our best. Or the other way I say this is:

I can't. He can. I will.

This is called 'Meekness.' Meekness is the realization of God's power and the fact that God's power resides in us, and He tells us to use said power to change our world.

This is God's only plan for redemption. There is no 'plan B.' Jesus hasn't come back to earth to share the gospel because we haven't.

It sounds like Joseph, in the Old Testament, saying: "Only God can interpret dreams…tell it to me."

It sounds like Peter, in Acts, saying: "We don't have silver and gold, but what we do have we will give you. In the name of Jesus rise up and walk."

Paul, former mass-murderer of Christians, still learned to say: "follow me while I follow Christ (1 Cor 11.1)."

The greatest joy you will have on earth is the life of discipleship you will have with those closest to you. Some people will come and go. Some will stay for a while. Some will never leave your side. Luke became that for Paul. Also note, Paul is getting a free trip to Rome paid for by the Roman government. God's provision doesn't always come on our terms.

Who discipled you, and whom are you discipling?

Day 9: Expect Opposition

Acts 27.1 When it was decided that we would sail for Italy, And embarking in an Adramyttian ship ... the winds were contrary, When we had sailed slowly for a good many days...

We've already established that God wants Paul to take Christianity to Rome. And what do we see the moment they hit the water? The winds were contrary...

A few entries later, we will see these 'contrary' winds are a massive storm. So why is it that whenever God sets destiny before us, there always seems to be opposition? Isn't God 'in-control?' Doesn't He have 'the whole world in His hands?' Hasn't he decreed everything 'from before the foundation of the earth?'

In a simple answer...no. God doesn't micro-manage the planet. Christianity is about 'agreeing with Jesus' and He teaches, if we encounter 'killing, stealing, or destroying' then that power comes from Satan. Our job is to fight back with 'abundant life (John 10.10).'

Jesus will call Satan 'god of this world.' The Greek word for 'god' here is 'archon', meaning 'local ruling authority.' God is the supreme authority over the whole universe for all time and eternity. But for a season, there is one small planet that has suffered a hostile takeover and is now ruled by a kidnapper.

Ok, I guess it wasn't that hostile of a takeover but it sure was thorough. Satan offered Adam and Eve the potential to be their own god and determine good from evil, right from wrong, and life from death for themselves. They loved the fact that now their only ruler was their comfort zone and pursuit of happiness.

God gave man rulership over the earth and didn't take it back when they fell. If a bully steals my son's baseball glove, I can do one of three things: I can go and buy my son a new glove and avoid the conflict. I, as a father, can go and beat up the bully and get the glove back. Or, I can take my son WITH me, and we can go and get the glove back.

Can you guess which option our heavenly Father chose? Eve was promised that her seed would crush the head of the serpent. Jesus is promised by God to sit at God's side until the enemy is made a footstool. Then, after the death, burial, resurrection, and Pentecost, Paul updates the thought as the conclusion to Romans by declaring: '**The God of peace will soon crush Satan under YOUR feet (Rom 16.20).**'

Whose feet? Ours. We get to Rome and crush Satan every step of the way. Just like Joshua walking into the promised land.

When have you encountered opposition in trying to follow Jesus?

Day 10: God Working in Spiritual Conflict

27.6 There the centurion found an Alexandrian ship sailing for Italy, and he put us aboard it. 7 When we had sailed slowly for a good many days, and with difficulty ...

Who saw God working? The first ship was not the ship Paul was supposed to pastor! They switched ships to ensure Paul reached more people than on the small boat they originally scheduled to take. This boat is a vast wheat shipping boat, as we will read later, and full of close to 300 men! What do we need to learn?

First, everyone on the planet will come against opposition in life. This is not an exclusively Christian problem. Buddhism's central tenant is that all life is suffering. 'Islam' literally means 'submission' to the will of Allah, good or bad. No one alive finds it easy to do the right thing or invest in the good of other people.

But...the uniqueness of the Wesleyan Christian perspective is that there is an active, aggressive force of evil on the planet called Satan. John's first letter sums up this perspective in two thoughts regarding God's nature and Jesus' assignment.

First, in regards to God's character, John states that God is light with NO variation (1 John 1.5). He also states that God is love (1 John 4.8). The love referred to here is agape love, which is other-centered, self-sacrificial love. In regards to Jesus' mission, John wrote the 'Son of God was revealed to destroy the works of the devil (1 John 3.8).' **Jesus did not come to destroy the works that God pre-determined people to do since before the foundations of the world! God doesn't play both sides of the chessboard.**

Yet, we can take courage that amid the battle, God is still working to maximize good and minimize evil. In this situation, Paul was getting to Rome, and the enemy was going to do everything He could to stop him.

So, what does God do? He makes sure Paul is going to have the biggest impact and gets him on a different boat. Did God know the sailing history of the captain? Did God know the greed of the boat owner? Did God hear the prayers of a mother who was praying for God's provision for one of her sons? Yes, and other things.

God doesn't 'cause all things.' He causes all things to 'work together' for good 1) FOR THOSE WHO love God and are 2) called according to HIS purpose. These two qualifiers must be met to walk in the peace that God is working, even when we can't see any signs of His work.

When have you seen God work amid a crisis?

Day 11: Waiting Longer...

27.7...since the wind did not permit us to go farther, we sailed under the shelter of Crete, ... and with difficulty sailing past it we came to a place called Fair Havens

What do you do when things don't change? Here in the story, Paul and friends aren't making any progress...or at least not quickly. Let's discuss what we do when we are contending for something and seeing nothing improve.

Most important is to not give up hope! Abraham is the father of faith because he **refused to waver** regarding God's promise. He knew God could produce what He promised (Rom 4).

The next thing is to reiterate what we went over the past few days; understand there is a spiritual battle going on. Don't be one of those Christians who always cry 'WHAT IS GOD DOOOOOING??' Easy, He is trying to mold you into looking like Jesus. News flash: Satan is trying to get you to look like Satan. Satan is terrified, anxious, bitter, and furious. He wants you to be as well.

The third idea is to use this waiting time to get as close to Jesus as you can. If there is a turbo boost in your Christian faith, it is when you make your best decisions on your worst days. When you act in faith even when you don't see God moving, you are lifting the heaviest weights while running an uphill marathon, into the wind while wearing high heels.

The sad part is most Christians never get to this point. They just say: 'it must be God's SAAAHHHHVREEN will.' And then instead of speaking to the mountain, they learn to camp on the mountain that God told them to move. All the while crying out to God: 'DON'T YOU CARE??' My belief is if you never grow past that attitude, God just looks at you and says: 'I'll wait.' He has time. He's already died on the cross, risen again and lives inside you. He's done His part. He refuses to do your part.

Remember, if you are having faith, you are winning. Faith is the substantiation of things hoped for. It's the number you put on the table while you wait for the pizza you've paid for. In having faith without sight, you are developing the very muscles that will help you LIVE blessed and not just experience a blessing. Faith only exists without sight. Faith IS the battle.

Then you express your faith through gratitude. Worship, sing, speak praises outloud, write gratitude lists. You will never know joy without gratitude.

If faith is the weight room, gratitude is the steroids. Doubt and negativity are the couch and giant bag of never-ending M and M's.

What are you having faith for right now?

Day 12: Wrong Season

27.9 When considerable time had passed and the voyage was now dangerous, since even the fast was already over, Paul began to admonish them...

If you read the statement 'after we opened everything under the tree, we went to the beach and went night swimming.' What conclusions would you draw?

Luke makes a similar statement: 'the voyage was now dangerous since even the fast was already over.' You can hear his slight emphasis 'even the fast was over.'

The expression 'the fast' would've been clear to the Jewish readers. The Day of Atonement was 'the fast.' Jewish believers every year fast for the forgiveness of their sins. This occurs in mid-September of every year.

What a modern reader won't get was sailing was dangerous from the end of July. By September it was impossible. Mid-September was a suicide mission. So these people who were as sea-faring as we are car driving are doing the math and saying 'Houston...we have a problem.'

What do you do when you are just in the wrong season to accomplish the things on your heart?

First, understand becoming Christ-like is not a calendar. Every day, every circumstance, each moment is a chance to learn to love Jesus more and then turn that love into service to the people around you. You may not be 'in Rome,' but you are becoming the person you need to be when you do arrive.

Second, understand if you are seeking God's kingdom and not your comfort, God may have some chess pieces to move before you can move forward. Before I became pastor of my church, God had to move on a pastor named Nate, to want to hire a pastor named Joe, to create the vacancy I filled. My 'suddenly' being asked to pastor took years of me knowing nothing. My job was to pray and be ready.

The third point to appreciate is God is working in everyone's life to get them to make better decisions. Everyone you are praying for has just as much stubbornness and free will as you did. God did not choose to make robots; He chose to raise children that learn to agree with Him. We may pray 'God ZAP them into obedience,' but He never will. That would be unloving, and God is love.

Bottom line, the wrong season is the perfect season to grow close to Jesus. When you commit to internal change, you become the person in whom God wants to make external changes.

So, start becoming the person you'll need to be in Rome.

Where can you grow in Jesus-likeness today?

Day 13: Pastor Your Shipwreck Before the Wreck

9 Paul began to admonish them,... "Men, I perceive that the voyage will certainly be with damage and great loss"

Here we get to the central theme of the booklet: Pastor your shipwreck.

Paul is on his journey to Rome but still realizes that his present job is to help everyone on the boat become more like Jesus. He takes a level of responsibility and starts to address the group.

But...don't forget...Paul is a prisoner on this boat. Of all the people on this ship, the person in chains, on his way to judgement, and potentially prison, isn't high on the list of voices that should be heeded. Right?

Never forget that the Spirit of God inside you is all the validation you ever need to speak on behalf of God! You and Christ in you are a majority.

Most people live with a validation deficit. This is why arrogance and selfishness are such common foes in our spiritual growth. We feel insecure and therefore need to validate ourselves or be validated by others. But remember, we are simultaneously the chosen son of God and deeply loved bride! There is no condemnation nor shame anywhere in our Spirit because, at our very core, is the Spirit of God.

When we realize how empowered we are, we no longer need to live desperately needing the validation, recognition affirmation, or celebration of others. We have all of that from Jesus!

Did you get that? You do not need validation from the opposite sex, from your parents, from your peers, from the media, from crowds, or from your bank account.

When that thought starts to gain traction, you can finally get set free from intimidation and the need to get a fix from everyone around you. **If you need other people to help you feel better then they become your drug! And you can't love them because you are too busy manipulating them.**

With all this said, we walk humbly, acknowledging that it is the life of Jesus working within us that gives us any empowerment to invest in the lives of others. But…if we take this passage seriously; we must conclude that even if I am the 'least likely to be listened to,' I am still positioned by Jesus to be His conduit of life, love, and power to all those whom I come into contact.

So disregard the chains on your wrists and focus on the Spirit within…you have a shipwreck to pastor!

Whom in my world needs more of my investment?

Day 14: Be a Prophetic Voice

27.10 "Men, I perceive that the voyage will certainly be with damage and great loss, not only of the cargo and the ship, but also of our lives."

Paul, in this passage, has discerned some bad news and isn't afraid to share this information. This present course of action is going to result in a disaster. He is acting as God's voice to those around Him. So what does it mean to live prophetically?

Keith Green wrote an article in the early '80s entitled, 'So you think you are a prophet?' This set off a huge discussion in the American church, over whether there were modern-day prophets or not. Sadly, a majority of that discussion revolved around the attitude and style of the person who believed they were being 'prophetic.' They thought if you were a 'prophet' you could get away with being abrasive.

Old Testament prophets had the Spirit of God 'upon' them and were the only people who were able to say, 'Thus sayeth the Lord.' If they were wrong, they were stoned immediately. Many people, like me, grew up with this style of prophetic word.

Our New Testament example of being a prophet is not John the Baptist, but Jesus. Whereas in the Old Testament the gift is <u>focused,</u> in the New Testament its <u>distributed</u>. We all have the gift of prophecy within us because we have the whole Holy Spirit within us. We develop the gift with use just like we develop specific muscles through use. My fork-lifting muscles are highly developed therefore the six-pack in my abs is therefore woefully underdeveloped.

Everyone in the New Covenant can and should hear and articulate God's voice to those around them. And they should do so from the fruit of gentleness whenever possible.

How do we grow in this gift? Easy, make a steadfast determination to memorize and utilize the words already revealed to us in the Bible. The more the **written** word of God flows in-and-out of your life, the more God can trust you with a **spontaneous** word from God.

Also, understand most of New Covenant prophecy is a reapplying of God's word like a parable to help people understand. The hope we should all live with is the belief that when we get in front of someone in need, we can trust that God will give us the words to share that will bring health, life, hope and healing.

When in your past, has someone shared a word from God to you that released life and hope?

Day 15: Expect *Not* to be Listened to

27.11 But the centurion was more persuaded by the pilot and the captain of the ship than by what was being said by Paul. 12 Because the harbor was not suitable for wintering, the majority reached a decision to put out to sea from there, if somehow they could reach Phoenix, a harbor of Crete, ... and spend the winter there.

You're going to notice a real pattern in this booklet. There is a spiritual battle and you should expect conflict every time you try to do something for Jesus. This entry has a couple of unique issues regarding other people.

Everyone has prayed for God to 'zap' another person into discipleship! Even if that person is us. Similarly, everyone has had to learn that a loving God will not choose to be unloving by unilaterally over-riding someone's free will. Drat that loving God giving people free will!

Can I help you understand the other reasons why? There are a few types of power. First, there is brute force power. I think we all agree God can but chooses never to use brute-force to get someone to love and obey Him. The second type of power is wisdom power. When a wise choice is suggested, a person's intellect is respected as they decide to choose or refuse the wise option. God loves to use this type of power and every parent out there knows how great it is when our children make a wise choice. Parents also know how excruciatingly long this process can take. Did you hear the root word 'cross' in the middle of 'excruciatingly?'

That is part of God's wisdom. **God wants people to function better and not merely feel better.** If God was to respond to every emotional demand we make, He would be teaching us that our emotions are the most essential part of us. So God patiently waits for us to understand the power of sowing and reaping. Eventually, our loved ones may choose the path of following Jesus.

Because that is the third type of power; Agape power. At some point, people become deeply attached to Jesus when they see how He patiently waits for us to make better choices. Then, when we have come to the end of ourselves, we aggressively choose to trust in the Lord with all our heart AND lean NOT on our own understanding. **The greatest thing I've learned in the past ten years is that my brain has been behind all of my worst ideas, and I can't afford to disagree with Jesus.**

The centurion and the voting crowd on the boat didn't listen to Paul. We didn't listen to Jesus the first few times either. The people we love won't listen to us all the time.

Have you ever had a 'rock bottom' moment?

Day 16: Bad to Worse

27.13 When a moderate south wind came up, supposing that they had attained their purpose, they weighed anchor and began sailing ...14 But ... there rushed down from the land a violent wind, ...and when the ship was caught in it... we gave way to it and let ourselves be driven along.

Today's entry will piggyback on yesterday's regarding how God wants people to learn the power of sowing and reaping.

I absolutely have set my life up to be a believer who walks in the supernatural power of God. I am not where I need to be, but am miles further down the road from where I used to be. Teaching people to pray-in miracles is one of the foundations of our church.

And...we don't see instant miracles all the time. For some, this is frustrating or proof that miracles don't happen anymore. I don't believe either of those thoughts because I understand God's commitment to the power of sowing and reaping.

Sowing and reaping is the foundation of every religion or philosophical belief on earth for all time. Seedtime and harvest are at the core of God's plan.

God wants every human to understand the power of sowing and reaping because when they start to follow

Him, they can use their will-power of sowing and reaping FOR GOOD and not for harm!

When my friends freak out about the poor choices their kids may be making, I try to calmly remind them that we also made bad choices. And this process is part of God teaching them to learn how to question their own thinking. That is called developing wisdom.

Discipleship takes place when we realize that our own brain has been behind every bad decision we have ever made, and we can't afford to disagree with Jesus.

The men on the boat didn't listen to Paul, and now they are heading towards a shipwreck. Our friends and loved ones are making bad choices and reaping the consequences. But, the heart of God's sovereignty is not in micro-managing the planet, but macro-managing to bring about good to those who love Him and are called according to HIS purposes. **All-powerful means all-resourceful, not all-controlling.**

So, whatever shipwreck your loved ones are in the midst of, we can be sure the wreck is NOT God's will. **But, their freedom to choose IS part of God's will!** Our privilege is to walk with them to help them realize that God can still bring good from whatever evil happens if they choose His way.

Who in your world is in the middle of reaping what they've sown?

Day 17: Peace in the Midst

27.18 ... we were being violently storm-tossed, they began to jettison the cargo; 19 and on the third day they threw the ship's tackle overboard with their own hands. 20 Since neither sun nor stars appeared for many days, and no small storm was assailing us, from then on all hope of our being saved was gradually abandoned.

Really read those verses. Can you hear the panic? They tossed the cargo and the ship's tackle overboard all with one hope; to live. This is easy to write off as something that happened to some people a long time ago. But to those on the boat, this is literally life and death. Do you hear the terror in verse 20? "From then on all hope...was gradually abandoned."

So how do we react in the middle of a crisis? How do we pray when we are terrified?

First, get to peace. When Jesus calmed the storm, He alone was able to sleep during the storm. You can only calm the storm you can sleep through. While all the disciples were screaming, 'we're dying!!!' Jesus was resting in the goodness of God. Yes, you may **be afraid,** but don't **live afraid!** Most of all, get to the point where you **are not praying afraid.**

Now, your emotions may be afraid, but remember your sprit is just fine, and that is the REAL part of you.

Second, don't pray the problem, pray the solution. Jesus woke up and told the situation what to do. It is still God's power that effects the change, but we are to act in faith before God moves. Remember, we don't tell God about the mountain; we tell the mountain about God. We have the keys of the kingdom and the authority to use them. If we don't use the keys, that isn't God's fault.

Third, get as thankful as possible. After we have prayed God's will for a situation, we need to water those seeds of prayer with the water of praise. When you praise God in advance, you are praising Him on credit. We are stopping our mouth from complaining about the reality of the problem and putting our words **by faith** in the reality of God's breakthrough power.

You go from addictive anxiety to powerful peace at the speed that God's impending intervention, is as real as your current crisis. If the problem you are facing is more powerful than God, go ahead and panic and go back to your addictions.

My guess is while everyone else is doing what they can do, Paul is crying out to God to do what He can do. We can't do God's part, and He refuses to do our part. We instigate divine intervention and praise Him in advance.

Where do you need to start praising God in advance?

Day 18: Prevail in Prayer

27.21 When they had gone a long time without food, then Paul stood up in their midst and said, "Men, you ought to have followed my advice and not to have set sail from Crete and incurred this damage and loss. 22 Yet now I urge you to keep up your courage, for there will be no loss of life among you, but only of the ship.

My late wife used to have a 'told-you-so' dance where she would move her hands like a flapper girl from the 20's while singing: told you...told you...told you so...

I doubt Paul had a similar dance but who knows...

Nevertheless, we will see Paul's heart in action in this passage. And if you look closely, you will see a miracle.

So the passage starts with stating that they have been in this storm a long time and they are so tossed around no one dares eat. Paul states the obvious about not listening to him and then starts to pastor his shipwreck.

"Keep your courage!" Jesus' peace is closer to courage than calmness. It is **fixing your eyes** and being **filled with peace** before it ever becomes **feeling peaceful**. Courage is where peace and faith dance together.

Then Paul makes a prophetic declaration: 'there will be no loss of life.' Did you notice the miracle?

In verse ten, Paul states that there will be loss of life. Now, in verse twenty-two, he says there will be no loss of life. What happened? Did God's will change??

No, God's will was enforced! It was never God's will for all of these people to die, since most of them would've gone into eternity in hell. Paul prayed until he PREVAILED in prayer. Anyone can say prayers. Only those with the heart of Jesus and the tenacity of Jesus can regularly prevail in prayer.

Prayer is not praying what we want; Prayer is praying what GOD wants and staying in the attitude of prayer until God's will is done ON earth, and ON our shipwreck as it is IN heaven.

Jesus accomplished God's will on the cross and then handed over the job of enforcement to those who would follow Him. And to ensure they had the requisite power, Jesus came and moved into them on the Day of Pentecost.

Now, we can do what Paul did, we can discern God's heart and go before His throne and insist on God's highest will in our world. And if you wonder what God's will is, just start by praying that everyone looks more like Jesus. That prayer will lead you to God's heart every time.

How does the concept of prevailing in prayer challenge what you think about prayer?

Day 19: Know Whose You Are

27.23 For this very night an angel of the God to whom I belong and whom I serve stood before me, 24 saying, 'Do not be afraid, Paul; you must stand before Caesar; and behold, God has granted you all those who are sailing with you.'

We are going to look at this verse for a couple of days.

The first thing I want you to notice is Paul knew how to keep praying until he received his breakthrough. God sent an angel to get the message through. Not bad.

So how do we get that kind of answer? Well, I can't speak to the angelic visitation, but I think the next sentence gives some idea of the type of praying that moves heaven and earth.

Paul says unequivocally that his life and destiny are in the hands of God and God alone. "Whom I belong" focuses attention on Paul's sense of identity. Paul is not a man in charge of his own destiny. He celebrates being 'owned' if you will, by God. Humans fight for their freedom every time they feel the need. Paul does the opposite; he celebrates the fact that he 'belongs' to God.

The book of Romans opens with Paul introducing himself as a bondservant. In Ephesians, chapter four, Paul calls himself a prisoner of the Lord. Those titles that humans are ashamed of, Paul claims with great pride!

The second thought is that he serves the God to whom he belongs. Humans seek their status by how many people serve them. Jesus and Paul turn that concept upside-down and declare the privilege of being the one who serves.

Just before the cross, Jesus gave His greatest lesson as He washed the feet of His disciples and told them to do the same. In the kingdom economy, servants are the ones with the power. Those who give up their life find it and those who die, walk in resurrection life.

No matter where you came from or what trauma you were marked by, your destiny is secure in the hands of Jesus, if you insist on being the servant. You can look back at your past and say: **'it might have shaped me, but it didn't define me!'** Your path of kingdom service is the path towards kingdom power.

The more you see your life and destiny in the hands of Jesus, to be lived-out in service to those around you, the more your praying will usher in the resurrection power of God. And your life, and the lives of those around you will never be the same.

Who are you serving and who do you need to start serving?

Day 20: Assume Responsibility

27.23 For this very night an angel of the God to whom I belong and whom I serve stood before me, 24 saying, 'Do not be afraid, Paul; you must stand before Caesar; and behold, God has granted you all those who are sailing with you.'

Do you notice the destiny connection in verse 24?

'You must stand before Ceaser...and...God has granted you all those...'

In God's eyes, your destiny is about you and those you serve. This is the crux of this booklet, and I'd argue the crux of the Christian message.

You become Christ-like, and lead everyone around you into Christ-likeness.

I should quit writing right now. Paul had to get to Rome as a part of His destiny, AND he was to accept responsibility for all of those around him.

I'm reminded of the life of Joseph, who just assumed that he was responsible for providing for the entire family THAT TRIED TO KILL HIM!

How was Joseph able to go from victim to hero? He saw God as in control of his destiny, and he learned to forgive. In Genesis 41, He named his sons 'God has caused me to forget the pain of my childhood' and

'God has made me fruitful in the land of my affliction (Gen 41.52).' Do you see God as the central thought in both of those declarations?

Joseph was able to reframe his trauma with a frame that pointed to God's faithfulness over men's evil. THAT is the spiritual movement which creates believers who are both no longer trapped in the evil they survived but also become sources of light and life to all they encounter.

Paul just assumed if you are somewhere in his world, he will make sure you get pulled **toward** God, when all your circumstances would make you want to **run from** God.

Assuming responsibility doesn't mean you take responsibility for everyone's bad choices. You just acknowledge that if someone is in your world, it is your job to pray for them. They still have enough willpower to destroy themselves, but you will use your willpower to pray. This way, you can always feel you are doing your part even if those around you are self-destructing.

Remember, if your preferred future doesn't have kingdom sacrifice at the center then you and God don't have the same preferred future in mind.

Do you see your destiny as being about bringing your world to the foot of the cross?

Day 21: Deliver the Good and the Bad

27.25 Therefore, keep up your courage, men, for I believe God that it will turn out exactly as I have been told. 26 But we must run aground on a certain island."

I love this passage. Talk about building everyone's hopes and then dashing them… or did he?

I can almost hear Paul saying somewhere before verse 25 'I have good news…and bad news.' We've all had those conversations.

And wouldn't you know that there is a tremendous spiritual insight in these verses?

If you look back in this booklet, you will notice I encourage everyone to be the prophetic voice to their world. Remember, New Testament prophecy isn't a 'for-telling' as much as it is a 'forth-telling.' Yes, there will be elements of predictions, but most prophecy in the New Testament era is about telling people what God has already said that applies to the current situation. Less 'thus sayeth the Lord' and more 'the kingdom of God is like…'

Paul sums up prophecy in 1 Cor 14.1 and 2 as being 'edification, encouragement and exhortation.' I like to sum this up as God's heart in your words. Also remember, that Paul links pursuing spiritual gifts and prophecy as much as we pursue love. And no one would argue against the fact that love is at the core of Christianity.

In these verses, Paul gives the good news that everyone will live while simultaneously preparing everyone for the shipwreck. Friends, can you see that as a microcosm of all of Christianity? You will survive and someday spend eternity with Jesus. Until then, there will be many shipwrecks.

These two thoughts, you WILL have tribulation, and Jesus has overcome the world are the railroad tracks of Christian sanity. The train moves just fine as long as those two thoughts stay apart and don't move. That is the tension we live in on this side of eternity.

God is God of the whole universe for all eternity, and Satan currently has homecourt advantage. The thief comes to steal, kill, and destroy while Jesus and His disciples come to bring abundant, miracle-filled life.

Some miracles will come quickly, and they will build your faith. Some miracles will be excruciatingly slow and will build your faith and character.

And we keep moving forward...rejoicing...loving the fight. Until we love fighting the devil, he loves fighting us.

What battle are you in that has good news and bad news?

Day 22: Hold on tight

27.27 But when the fourteenth night came, ... about midnight the sailors began to surmise that they were approaching some land. ...29 Fearing that we might run aground somewhere on the rocks, they cast four anchors from the stern and wished for daybreak.

So what do we do when we are about to enter into a shipwreck. Cast some anchors and wait for daybreak.

This is so important; this could be the thought that gets you out of a lifetime of anxiety. **Refuse to be a victim of your own thinking!**

Your mind is stronger than your brain. Every morning you get 3,000,000 new brain cells to reprogram. They WILL be programmed either with past patterns or new healthy thoughts, based on the word and faithfulness of God. This is what Paul calls 'renewing your mind' and 'taking every thought captive.' Christian history and David in the Psalms call this 'meditation.'

Biblical meditation is not like Eastern religion's meditation. In Eastern religions, meditation is about emptying your mind. Biblical meditation is fixing or focusing your mind on the word.

Just like the boat was anchored as the storm started to hit, you need to learn to meditate BEFORE you get into the storm.

Start with worship music. Become obsessed to surround yourself with songs of God's faithfulness.

Next, make sure you have written down all the miracles you've experienced. This should be a section in every prayer journal.

Have a list handy of all the facts that are true about you because Jesus lives in you. The appendixes in the back of this book contain much of this information.

Finally, get completely convinced you will grow through this shipwreck. You, your family, your loved ones will all benefit from what God is getting you through.

After these things are in place, start to praise God in advance. Declare God's will over each situation, and don't be afraid to pray huge, God-honoring prayers. God's goal in any of these situations is to get you through this 'red sea' circumstance and leave you free, and your enemies drowned! Praising God in advance is how you go offensive in your prayer life, as opposed to staying defensive. This is what it looks like to run toward Goliath, as David did.

What could God be working in you during this current crisis you are fighting?

Day 23: Pastor Your Shipwreck!

27.30 The sailors were trying to escape …Paul … "Unless these men remain in the ship, you yourselves cannot be saved." … Paul was encouraging them all to take some food, saying, "Today is the fourteenth day …going without eating, … take some food, …for not a hair from the head of any of you will perish." 35 …he took bread and gave thanks to God … and he broke it and began to eat. 36 All of them were encouraged and they themselves also took food. 37 All of us in the ship were two hundred and seventy-six persons.

We are now getting to the crux of the story. Paul becomes the pastor of this group of almost three hundred people.

The passage starts with some of the crew planning their escape. They planned to cut loose and try to survive on a smaller dinghy.

While this is happening, Paul is standing as the living contrast to the panic of the crewmen. The rest of the ship is so seasick, that they haven't eaten in TWO WEEKS! They are weary and terrified. Paul is starting to discern where the problem is going and what needs to be done so that everyone survives.

Paul starts by telling them to eat and gain their strength while reminding them that they will all survive. Doesn't this sound like Joseph in Genesis?

Joseph discerned both the problem and what should be done simultaneously.

God wants you to have that type of relationship with God AND with people. We stay connected vertically with God and horizontally with people.

And to bring all this together, Paul serves communion. Just like before Jesus went to the cross, He didn't preach a sermon…he offered a dinner.

Friends, this is the crux of pastoring your shipwreck and changing your world. You stand with one hand holding onto God and one hand holding onto the hands of those you love. This way, when people are in crisis, they have you to turn to until they can turn to God directly.

"Follow me while I follow Christ." This is what Paul writes to the Corinthians. We get to Rome. We expect storms, we expect the ship to wreck and we will pastor everyone around us on the way.

There is no plan 'B.' God is not doing a 'new thing.' He is trying to get believers to do what He has told them to do since Eden. Agree with Jesus, serve like Jesus, heal like Jesus.

Change your world like Jesus.

Who in your shipwreck is closest to accepting Jesus?

Day 24: God Never Promised the Boat

27.39 They could not recognize the land; ... they resolved to drive the ship onto ... they ran the vessel aground; ... the stern began to be broken up by the force of the waves. 42 The soldiers ... commanded that those who could swim should jump overboard first and get to land, 44 and the rest should follow, some on planks, and others on various things from the ship. And so it happened that they all were brought safely to land.

Take a deep breath. This might get tough.

God never promises the boat that will get you to Rome. He only promises you will get there.

Why is this tough? Because **we have invested most of our lives in our boats.**

So, when the shipwrecks come, we cry out to God 'don't you care??'

But God never promises the ship.

This first impacted me when all of my best friends, who made up the best worship team in town, all left my church at once.

The 'boat' of this group of friends, and huge influence in my life, had some shipwrecks in their lives and moved on. Now I was left alone holding onto my plank in the midst of a storm.

Then a few years later, my lovely wife of 26 years passed away. Now, of ALL the ships I thought would survive the trip to Rome, I was SURE my marriage would survive the storm.

When you learn to trust God more than any boat you encounter, and / or build, you will truly learn about faith. You need to hold onto the goodness of God amidst a fallen planet like Paul hung onto a plank from the boat while floating to shore. And I am guessing Paul was singing 'THIS IS THE DAY! THIS IS THE DAY THAT THE LORD HAS MADE...'

That is how we pastor our shipwreck. **We become radically convinced that God is always good, this planet is always a war zone, and we are destined to always triumph in Christ Jesus** (2 Cor. 2.14).

Always triumph doesn't mean every victory will be 100 to 0. It means we have an eternal perspective that as long as we plant the seeds of faith, we will always see God's hand at work. When we continually choose to step closer to Jesus in the midst of everything, we can be assured that God hasn't quit working. Our job is to never say ANYTHING Jesus wouldn't say... and grab a plank.

What shipwrecks have you survived?

Day 25: It's OK to Just Survive

27. 43 but the centurion, wanting to bring Paul safely through, kept them from their intention, and commanded that those who could swim should jump overboard first and get to land, 44 and the rest should follow, some on planks, and others on various things from the ship. And so it happened that they all were brought safely to land.

Sometimes it's all you can do to grab a plank and start kicking towards the shore. Survival is better than the alternative.

Right now as I write this in May of 2020, the world is still in the grips of COVID 19. While I haven't lost anyone and only know one friend-of-a-friend who contracted the virus, I have lost three people to suicide and two more attempted suicide. While talking to the people in my city, the speculation is wild in every direction. The uncertainty about many issues is trying to steal everyone's peace.

So what does someone do when they have zero control and some very dangerous circumstances overhead? **You grab a plank and kick toward the shore.** I wish I could be more pithy or insightful, but sometimes living to see another day is all we can hope for.

But...Remember one thing: the skills you develop in trying to survive will sabotage any attempt to thrive. Survival demands you eliminate vulnerability. Thriving is contingent on having appropriate levels of vulnerability and an outlook that is anticipating blessing. If you live in survival mode, always waiting for the other shoe to drop then you will never develop the requisite peace that leads to the blessed life Jesus desires for us.

Jesus models for us that, self-sacrificial love is stronger than death. For a person in survival mode, being vulnerable sounds like a fate worse than death. So what do you do while you are holding onto your plank and kicking towards the shore? You worship in advance.

In my mind, Paul is singing 'THIS IS THE DAY...THIS IS THE DAY...THAT THE LORD HAS MADE...' the entire time he is floating. How can I believe that? Because Paul and Silas worshipped the prison walls down a few stories earlier. Worshipping God in advance is like thanking Him on credit. God will not be in 'worship-debt' to anyone. Plus, this positions your spirit to be ready to see God's breakthrough in the midst.

I would also encourage you to regularly reframe the survival stories as stories of God's faithfulness. **God sustained you even if you felt He failed you**. This will start you moving from survival to thrive-al.

What survival stories need to be reframed as stories of God's faithfulness in your past?

Day 26: Go Serve

28.1 When they had been brought safely through, then we found out that the island was called Malta. 2 The natives showed us extraordinary kindness; ... they kindled a fire and received us all. 3 But when Paul had gathered a bundle of sticks and laid them on the fire

I. Love. This.

They kick onto the shore, holding onto the scraps of the ship that just disintegrated around them. Its raining and cold, and Paul...gets out of the water and volunteers to gather wood.

Friends, there is no shortcut to spiritual maturity. There is, however, a turbocharge button. A Saab turbo button of course.

'**Make your best choice on your worst day.**' That is how you turbo-boost your faith. In this situation, I believe Paul worshipped in the sea as he did in jail. Then when he got to the shore, He decided that it was his job to serve everyone around him.

Everything in the kingdom is upside down. The God of the universe accomplished His highest priority by sneaking into the womb of a scared teenage girl...so He could DIE! Paul will later write in Philippians that Jesus humbled Himself first, THEN God highly exalted Him. Jesus was servant and then Lord in that order.

This is the great scandal of the cross and faith: **at the cross we see God dying at the hands of man to show God's undying love for man**. We may love the fact that God is still on the throne…but remember, God on a cross is just as Biblical.

What did Jesus do before He went to the cross? He washed their feet and told them to do the same. And then He went to the cross! When Jesus greeted His followers after the Resurrection when they had gone back fishing, He greeted them BY MAKING BREAKFAST!

Jesus had a bucket list…grab a bucket and wash feet. Jesus had a corporate ladder…and it led to the cross.

It doesn't matter what your home life was like; you can serve. It doesn't matter what your education level is; you can serve.

The most freeing, anti-anxiety thought you can hold is that Jesus alone holds your destiny. And you access that destiny every time you ask someone: 'Is there anything I can do for you?' Our world judges success by how many people serve you. Jesus judges success by how dirty and heroin-injected the feet are that you just finished washing.

So, leave your ship plank in the lake and go find some firewood.

Who are you serving for Jesus sake right now?

Day 27: Expect...

28.3 But when Paul had gathered a bundle of sticks and laid them on the fire, a viper came out ... and fastened itself on his hand. 4 When the natives saw ... they began saying to one another... this man is a murderer, and though he has been saved from the sea, justice has not allowed him to live." 5 However he shook the creature off into the fire and suffered no harm. 6 But they were expecting that he was about to swell up or suddenly fall down dead. But after they had waited a long time ... they changed their minds and began to say that he was a god.

Out of the fire and into the flame...out of the shipwreck and into the cold of night and the gossip of people.

If you remember the beginning of this journey, one of the key thoughts is on your journey to Rome...expect a shipwreck. Now that you've survived the shipwreck, you should expect to be snake bit, gossiped about, have people expect you to die, and then think you are a god.

The fight never ends if you are on the trip to Rome. If you are experiencing things like this, consider them as signs you are on the right path. When I drive from Spokane to Seattle, crossing the Columbia River and then the Cascade Pass, are signs I am on the right path.

I want to highlight one of these elements. When Paul got bitten by the snake, the people watching made a HUGE leap of logic in thinking that Paul was a murderer. Then they made a HUGE philosophical leap by deducing their god, called 'justice,' was behind the snake bite.

Our first point from this is: expect people to talk about you and expect you to die. People love to feel superior to the misfortunes of others. Again...consider this a sign you are on the right path.

But a more subtle point is this: Paul was a murderer. We know what to do when people talk about you and its not true. But what do we do when people talk about you...and it is true?

That will be tomorrow's entry.

But for now remember, if you feel that you are doing all you can to get to Rome, and every force on the planet is trying to stop you, and the people sent to help you are making things worse...**then you are probably on the right path**. Paul and Jesus can both attest to this reality. Just keep your eyes on Jesus, seek first the kingdom, grab a plank and shake off that snake!

When in your past, have people meaning to help you made things worse? Have you forgiven them? Are you making things worse for anyone in your world?

Day 28: Shake it off and Heal the City

28.5 However he shook the creature off into the fire and suffered no harm... (the mayor) of Publius was lying in bed afflicted with recurrent fever and dysentery; and Paul went in to see him and after he had prayed, he laid his hands on him and healed him. 9 After this had happened, the rest of the people on the island who had diseases were coming to him and getting cured. 10 They also honored us with many marks of respect; and when we were setting sail, they supplied us with all we needed.

The more obsessed you are with accomplishing all that Jesus has put in front of you, the less the enemy's attacks will stop you. AND you'll heal an entire city on the way.

This should make you jump up and dance the watusi!

When fear becomes fuel for faith, obstacles become catapults. Paul shakes off the snake because that snake **is not part of his destiny**. Paul ignores the gossiping because the opinion of others **is not part of his destiny**. The thinking that Paul was a god was also ignored by Paul because flattery **is not part of his destiny.**

My son said it best...when you say Jesus alone holds my destiny, you need to end the sentence with a period. If you end the sentence with an asterisk, implying there are other conditions, then Jesus does not hold your destiny.

To the degree Jesus <u>alone</u> holds your destiny is the degree you will walk in His power, peace, and joy. Fear dilutes faith. For most believers, we are trying to light a fire of faith while simultaneously pouring the water of fear on our fire, all while crying out 'God doesn't care.'

So if you get bitten by a snake and gossiped about by natives, take a deep breath and say 'who's sick? I must be here to see God heal people.'

Satan's greatest attack on God's plan was the crucifixion of Jesus. How well did that end for Satan? Until you love fighting the devil, the devil loves fighting you.

We have to become convinced that every shipwreck is preceding the healing of a city.

And you getting to Rome. Read this again:

Jesus alone holds my destiny.

Not

Jesus alone holds my destiny*

Where have you let fear dilute your faith because of circumstances?

Day 29: Love the Person Chained to You

28.14 There we found some brethren, and were invited to stay with them ... and thus we came to Rome... 16 When we entered Rome, Paul was allowed to stay by himself, with the soldier who was guarding him.

I can make a lot of things complicated. And I can hear you 'amen-ing' in the background as I draw this booklet to a conclusion.

This I can't complicate; living like Jesus means loving the person in front of you. In Paul's case, it was loving the centurion to whom he was chained.

How do we make sure we get to our Rome? How do we ensure we don't make wrong turns along the way?

Easy, you just wake up every morning and set your eyes to seeking first the Kingdom of God, which looks like loving the person in front of you.

Jesus says, in the Sermon on the Mount, that we should do unto others as we would have them do unto us. He then tells His listeners to not be like the crowd, which are seeking the easy path. Instead, seek the narrow path, the harder path. This should tell you everything you need to know.

Do you want people to pray for you? Pray for them. Do you want people to teach and disciple you? Teach and disciple those around you. Are you hoping people in your world, bless you on your path? Then you should do the same by serving those God puts in front of you.

In Paul's case, I believe he looked at every guard, that he was chained to, as being the next person who would hear about Jesus.

Never forget this, God's plan to win the whole world to Jesus, **is to look through your eyes and lead you to sacrificially love all those you see**. Every person is being drawn-in by the Father, and you get to have the honor of loving them to life.

Rome is ahead of you. Your destiny to live a full, joyful life means you will have many people to love like Jesus.

Think about your preferred future. In this future, are you loving people sacrificially as the main activity of your life? If you aren't…your preferred future doesn't line up with God's preferred future for you. If your vision mainly is about stuff, vacations, cars or acclaim, then you have just stumbled upon your idols.

You have survived enough shipwrecks. Now its time to thrive in the promised land God promised you!

Does your dream future include more Kingdom sacrifice? What does your vision include instead?

Day 30: Bound is Just a State of Mind

28.23 Wen they had set a day for Paul, they came to him at his lodging in large numbers; and he was explaining to them by solemnly testifying about the kingdom of God and trying to persuade them concerning Jesus, from both the Law of Moses and from the Prophets, from morning until evening...30 And he stayed two full years in his own rented quarters and was welcoming all who came to him, 31 preaching the kingdom of God and teaching concerning the Lord Jesus Christ with all openness, unhindered.

As we conclude, we see Paul in Rome, in his apartment, in the will of God. People from all over are coming to him to hear about Jesus. I am going to call this 'reverse missions.'

We are used to hearing 'going into all the world to make disciples.' Paul's unique circumstances doesn't hinder his preaching the word. God just turns the method upside down to fit His purposes.

Note, Paul is still under house arrest. I don't recommend this as your ministry strategy but look at how God turned this all for good.

Paul knew it was His assignment to take Christianity from obscure Nazareth to the center of the known world. He encountered being ignored, waiting, having the timing be wrong, finding small miracles, going through an actual shipwreck, swimming to shore, getting snake-bit, getting gossiped about, healing a city and now we see him having the whole city come TO him.

God causes all things to work together for good, FOR THOSE WHO love God (Paul does) and are called according to HIS purpose (the subject of this entire book).

When your heart is set to enforce Jesus' victory into those circumstances where it looks like the devil is winning, you position yourself to see radical miracles. But each step of the way, it will look like nothing is going right.

Every boxer knows that the knock-out punch is what the people remember. But a successful boxer knows that each individual body-blow wears-down the less successful boxer. And that sets up the spectacular knock-out punch. Keep punching. God causes us to 'always triumph' in Christ. And triumph looks like throwing a ton of body-blows.

I started the booklet quoting Jerry Cook and I'll let Him close. He says that God's plan is you, being you, filled with Him, open for business and doing today well. And that is how every victorious trip to Rome is won.

What area of your life has you throwing many body-blows?

Appendix 1

Why Journal?

If you've never journaled, allow me to invite you into one of the greatest activities with which a person can get involved.

Journaling is a spiritual discipline where each person takes their walk with Jesus seriously enough to create a tangible record. Now don't get intimidated! Journaling is as easy or as complex, as you wish to make it.

Journaling can be as easy as writing down a thought you read in scripture, a prayer request, and something for which you are thankful.

Journaling can be as complex as working through deeply held beliefs and struggles under the umbrella of prayer.

Your call. Remember, journal as you can... not as you can't.

A great starting place would be:

- Start with being thankful for a few specific things.
- Ask God to bring His will into specific situations on your heart.
- Ask God to fulfill any needs you may have.

If you have some issues in your character that may need God's touch, be sure to write those down to chart how far you have come.

Next, move to writing down a thought or two from your Bible reading that day. This booklet is designed to jump start your writing with stimulating subjects. If all fails, open up to the Psalms (usually right in the middle) and read until you find a verse that echoes your thoughts for the day.

You can be specific or general in your writing. You can even use codes if you fear someone reading them. Remember, you set the rules.

Now, if you really want to grow, be sure to tell people the good news you find. The fastest way to grow is to make a habit of telling people what you are learning on a daily basis. When I find something good, I try to tell five people that day. In Christianity, you only keep what you give away.

The most exciting part is when you look back and see how God has answered prayer, changed your character or seen how He has spoken to you while you were processing your thoughts.

Good luck and God bless!

Appendix 2

Picking a Bible

If you don't have a Bible, here are some great things to consider.

Each Bible translation tries to bring the ancient languages into modern English. That isn't a very easy task. There are two schools of thought about the best way to approach translation.

One school of thought is that the Bible should be as easily understandable today as it was to the first people who read the text. This approach will make reading easier to understand but may make some simplifications with the interpretation. This type of translation is called 'dynamic.' These Bibles are great to read.

The other school of thought is called 'literal.' Here the translators try to bring the English to be as close to the ancient Greek or Hebrew as possible. While the translation is accurate, the English can be stilted or tougher to understand. These Bibles are great to study.

Some thoughts on modern translations:

New International Version (NIV): by far the most popular for good reason. An accurate translation that is easy to understand.

New Living Translation (NLT): Very similar to the NIV, maybe even easier to read. Great for teens.

NIrV: An NIV written for people with a lower reading level. Great for kids.

New American Standard Bible (NASB): My favorite. A Painfully accurate translation. I used to correct my Greek homework by looking in the NASB. The new version for 2020 is a great improvement.

English Standard Version (ESV) : Great new translation that is 97% the same as the NASB with smoother English. May be the best of all worlds.

New King James Version (NKJV): Updated King James Version. Beautiful ancient English that might be tougher to understand but wonderful use of the English language.

So- that is a quick look at the modern translation. Pick one or two and jump in!

Appendix: Prayer tips

Prayer list:

I strongly recommend creating a prayer list of people and situations in your journal.

You don't have to follow the list, but if you are anything like me, you have had times where you sat down to pray and your mind goes blank.

This is why a list helps.

You don't have to feel tied to the list, but this will help you keep moving forward in prayer during those times your brain is not fully engaged. Your spirit is always engaged...your brain...not-so-much.

You can actually write down prayers for each person on your list, or just use the names to remind you to mention them in prayer.

Prayer times:

Jesus prayed both early and late. I'm guessing through the day as well.

Currently with my wacky schedule I have six times during my day where I can fit in 15-20 minutes in prayer. If I make three of those times in a day, I feel pretty good.

I try to make sure that I spend at least one of those times in my prayer language and one of those times journaling.

Those are my set times; I also try to steal times. Stolen times are when you are praying while doing something else. Time in the shower or car are great opportunities. But remember... my stolen times are better when I am making my set times.

If all you are trying to do is steal time or pray on the run, I fear you may not have made prayer a real priority. We come to God for salvation on His terms. We should avoid coming to Him for prayer on our terms.

Praying in your mind, as the day goes on, is closer to meditation than intercession. Meditation is a good practice and certainly better than using your mind to rehearse old grievances or the state of the Mariner's bullpen. But...I don't think all of heaven jumps to attention when you worry and occasionally say God.

Bill Johnson famously said, "If your prayer doesn't move you, why do you think it will move God?"

I believe intercession starts when your world stops. If you had waited six months to get in with a brain surgeon, would you have your phone on, Grey's Anatomy on, your lap top open and be plucking your eyebrows during the meeting?

Meditation:

Meditation is God-focused thinking. Eastern meditation is about emptying yourself to join with a cosmic one-ness. Christian meditation is focusing your mind on the truth of God to allow His word to take root in your spirit.

Silent prayer would or should fall in this category. When we meditate, we give God the reigns to our mind and we make mental / spiritual connections to the truths we are focusing on.

I will take a verse, story or song and just chew on it all day and watch what God brings to the surface. Eighty-five percent of what I preach on any given Sunday has come from my meditation time.

This is also where most of my analogies come from. Last night while I was meditating on my dog walk, my dog bolted away because she smelled something. Meditation is like that...you will start meditating on a subject, and God will drop a thought into your brain and you will mentally pursue the thought like my dog did the smell. This is a huge way to integrate the truth of God's word into the day-to-day of life. What you focus your mind on, you empower. If you focus on worry you empower fear. If you focus on God's truth, you empower Him. One brings anxiety...the other brings peace.

Hearing God's Voice:

While there is a chapter on this, let me add a few more thoughts.

The first and easiest way for God to speak to you is through worship music. When a song comes into your brain GRAB IT! This is the voice of God!

If you wish to grow in this gift, take apart that song as a meditation exercise. For example, if "Jesus Messiah" comes to mind, I will think: 'He became sin who knew no sin... what sins of mine did He take to the cross? Am I getting free from them?'

'Name above all names... One of God's names is Jehovah-Jireh: God will provide. The word says that at the feet of Jesus every knee will bow... so I speak to my fear of poverty and command it to bow its knee at the feet of Jesus.'

See how I took the thoughts of the song and made them real in my life? If you show God you are serious about hearing His voice He will speak more.

The last thought about hearing God's voice is the more scripture you have in your brain, the more God will bring to your attention, and the more you will discern how precise you are in hearing His voice. Without a doubt or qualification, the most prophetic people I have ever known are the people who know the Word the best. God will NEVER contradict His revealed word with a prophetic word.

So find a verse, or worship song and let it take over your mind for a day!

Appendix 4
Statements of Agreement

After Lynne died, I made sure I read my statements of agreement at least once a day. Remember, these statements are true, whether you agree or not! You might as well agree with who Jesus says you are.

I AM in Jesus and Jesus is in me.
I AM a new creation. Old things are gone and ALL things are being made new!
I AM Jesus' representative to my world.
I AM focused on my Father's business.
I AM God's work of art, created for the work of God.
I AM Ready for ALL the Holy Spirit has for me!
I AM an empowered vessel of the Holy Spirit.
I AM a loved child of God, and He is proud of me!
I AM driven and fed by God's work in my world.
I AM solely empowered by serving like Jesus.
I AM led by God's plan every day!
I AM a vessel of the Holy Spirit's power.
I AM God's agent of reconciliation.
I AM the instigator of Divine Intervention!
I AM empowered to bring healing!
I AM Jesus' fisherman to my world. My joy and peace is the bait and His love is the hook.
I AM empowered to heal and I AM growing in wholeness based on my time alone in God's presence.

I AM the carrier of faith for my world. And if need be, I will carry my friends and tear off roofs!
I AM pure before God so God's power can flow purely through me.
I AM God's bridge into the lives of those I love.
I AM capable of starving my flesh to strengthen my spirit through fasting.
I AM living out of my new thinking and not my old neediness!
I AM a person who invests time in Sabbath life, because that empowers the rest of the time in my life.
I AM healed, filled, and empowered to walk out the life Jesus has poured in!
I AM empowered to be God's answer to life's problems.
I AM blessed because of my Kingdom investment of service.
I AM empowered by my self-sacrifice.
I AM an investor of the life of Jesus.
I AM the carrier of God's will for everyone who I contact.
I AM fruitful in every endeavor of my life!
I AM all Jesus says I am.
This journal is my prophetic title deed and I will see everything written in here.
I am a kingdom seeker, a foot washer.
I lay hands on the sick and they recover.
I cast out demons with a word and they stay out.
I curse unfruitful things and they die.
I speak to dry bones and they live.
I speak to mountains and they move.
I can do all things because I can seek first.

The loudest voice in my head is not God but I am making 'I am blessed even when it doesn't look or feel like I am blessed' louder every day.
I have an anointing that abides.
I am growing in character, growing in power, and hearing God's voice better every day.
I am preparing to do the greater works Jesus promised.
I go into all the world, and make disciple-making disciples.
I love fighting the devil, and love enforcing God's will, I feed and am sustained by seeing God's will.
I grow stronger as I pray longer because what God promised He can produce.
I do not grow weary in well doing, I get stronger day by day.
I know God's working for my good because I love Him and am seeking His purpose.
I am a co-heir with Jesus, am seated in high places with Jesus.
Greater is the Spirit within me then everything in the world.
No weapon formed against me will succeed and everything that comes against me is accursed.
I am blessed by God and cannot be cursed.
I am crucified with Christ and Christ lives through me.
I am undefeatable because the life of Jesus flows through the wounds of this life.
I am a new creation, everything in me is being made new.
I am free of hurts and wounds of my past.
I am free of demonic chains.
I am free of bitterness and unforgiveness.
I am on a path that shines fuller like a sunrise.

I am a son of God and part of the bride of Christ.
I was purchased by and am perfected by the blood of Jesus.
I am filled with abundant life as I carry my cross and put my flesh to death.
There is no shame anywhere in me.
I need no recognition, affirmation, validation or celebration from anyone because I have those things from Jesus.
I am the healthiest soil I have ever been and am walking into my most fruitful season ever.
I WILL (future) be as fruitful in (desired fruitfulness) as I currently am in (current fruitfulness).
- For me
    I will be as fruitful in healing as I am in humor.
    I will be as fruitful in deliverance as I am in delivering a sermon.
    I will be as fruitful in salvations as I am at playing musical instruments. ETC

I walk and live in the fruitfulness, joy and peace given to me by Jesus.
I have the keys to the kingdom and am not afraid to use them. I bind that which is bound in heaven and I release that which has been released in heaven.
My peace calms storms because the peace empowering me is stronger than the fear crushing me.
No weapon formed against me will prosper.
I bring living water to my world.
I bear in my body the death of Jesus so the life of Jesus flows to my world.
I fix my eyes on invisible eternal realities.
I give every spiritual gift.
I have the breakthrough anointing.
My prayer language is my:

> Prophetic breakthrough battering ram
> Guarantee of 'greater things' and God's will
> Praying to God the alphabet so He can write my story.

I advance as I invest.
I covet no ones: (fill in your own blanks)
There are more for me than against me.
I do not want others to be envious of me.
I am safe in the Father's love
> Strong in Jesus name
> Significant by the power of the Spirit

The more I seek, the more God sends.
I AM NOT A VICTIM OF MY OWN THINKING
I Desire God's life through me more than the good life around me.
I am free, favored, fruitful!
My past shaped me; it didn't define me.
Jesus alone holds my destiny and future.

About the Author

Pastor Sean Lumsden graduated from Azusa Pacific University in 1992 with a Bachelor's Degree in Theology and a Minor in Biblical Greek.

These degrees were immediately put to use as Sean started in an 18 year career as a waiter.

In 1996, Sean was licensed as a Pastor from the International Church of the Foursquare Gospel. Shortly after, he planted "jacob's ladder" one of the first 'Gen-x' churches in the nation. Not a particularly large church, their slogan was "come to jacob's ladder and get alone with God."

Eventually Sean and his family went to Spokane, Washington where Sean helped start a few churches. Additionally, he worked as a financial planner, national-award winning advertising copywriter, radio disc-jockey, music instructor and again as a waiter.

Currently, Sean is the pastor of Living Hope Foursquare, a funky little church in a funky part of Spokane. At Living Hope, their church aims to make people 'Jesus-ish'. Their slogan is 'creating Christ-like people who love people like Christ.'

On December 27, 2018, Sean's beloved wife of 25 ½ years, Lynne, passed away. Lynne's passionate commitment to better the lives of deaf people was an inspiration to everyone she met. She became the top sign-language interpreter in the country while battling mental health issues. Sadly, those issues caught up with her and led to her early death.

Sean still writes commercials while he pastors, and in his spare time he hangs out with his family, collects musical instruments, plays tennis and takes his Saab into the shop for repairs.

You can contact Sean at PastorSean@LivingHopeSpokane.com.

Made in the USA
Middletown, DE
21 October 2022